I0797453

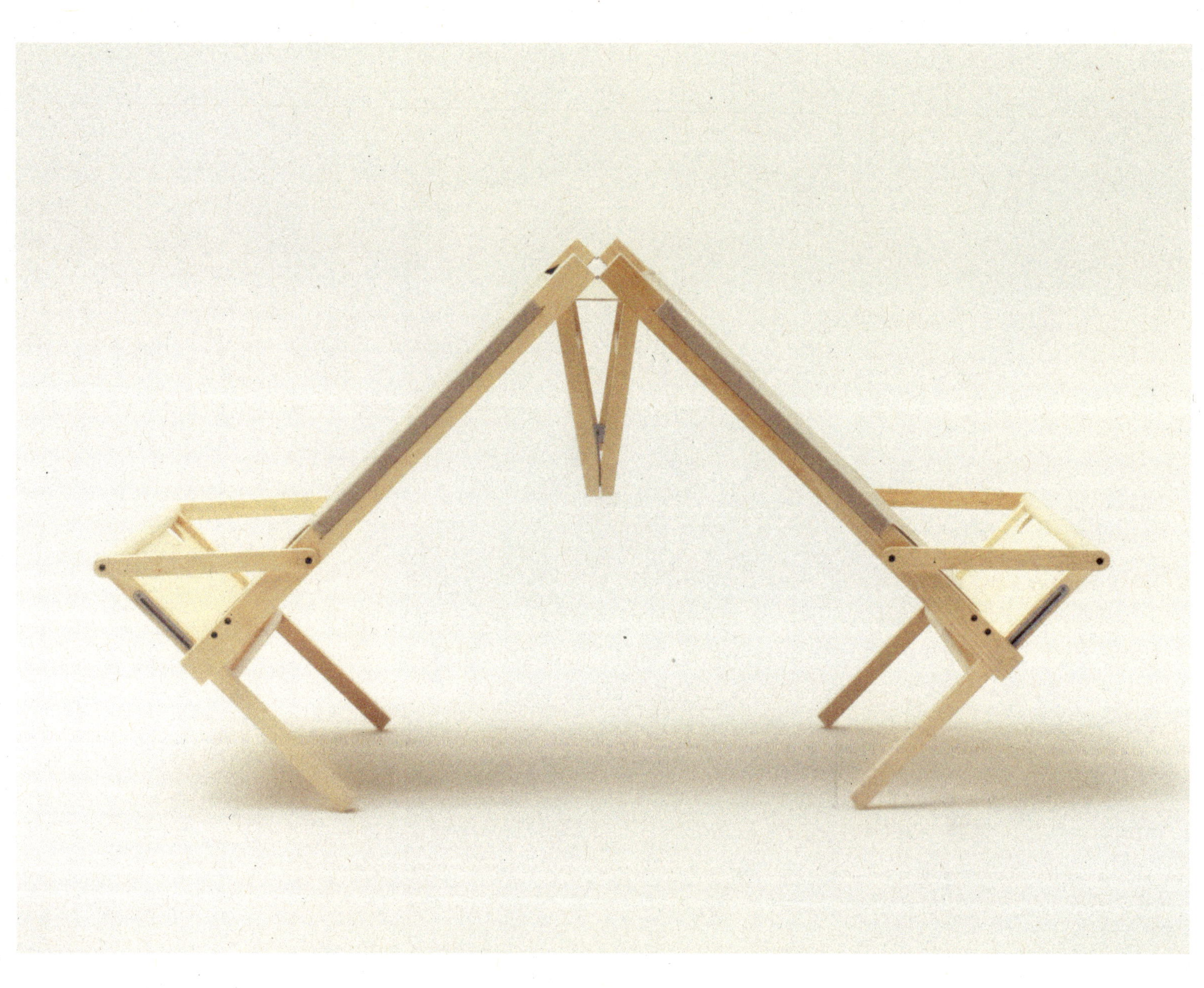

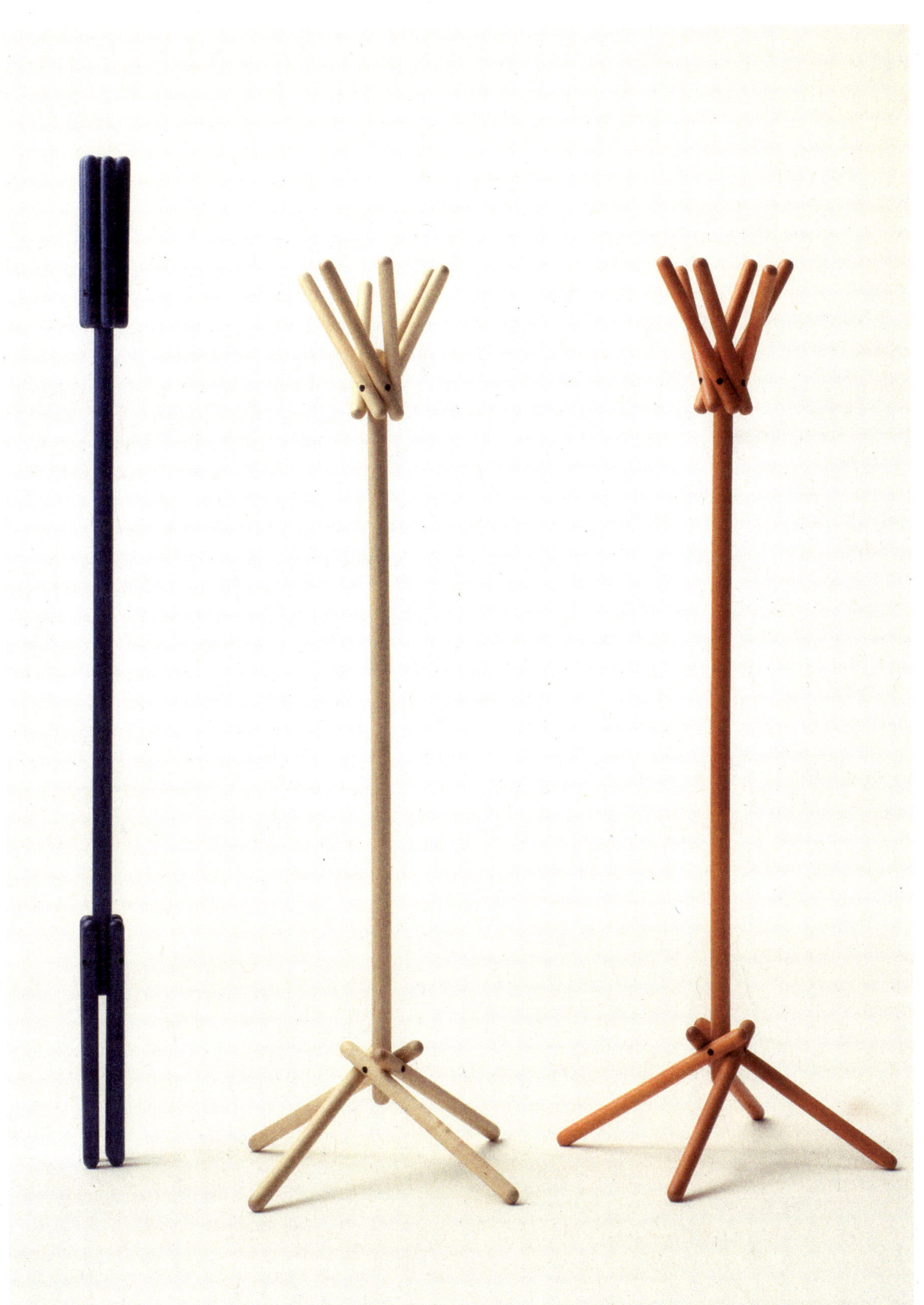

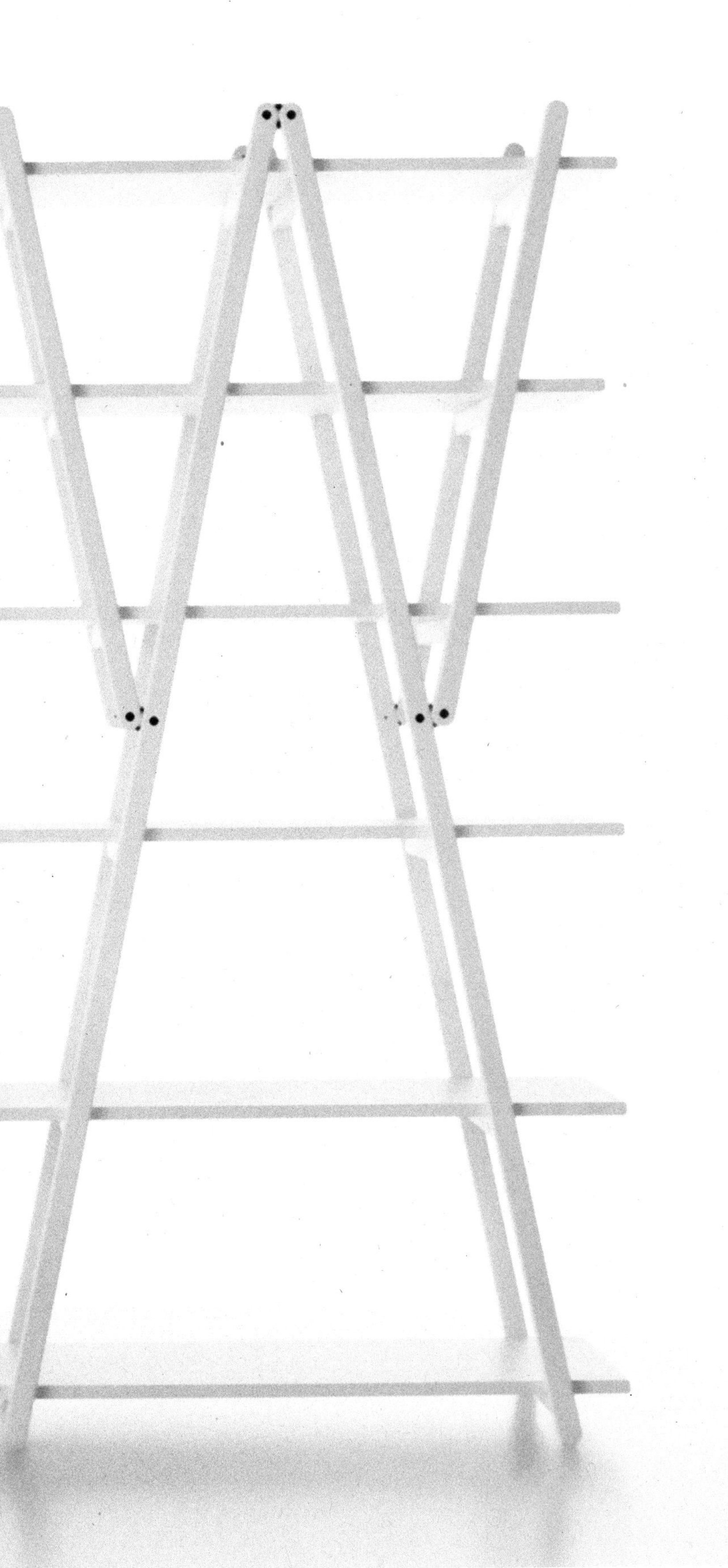

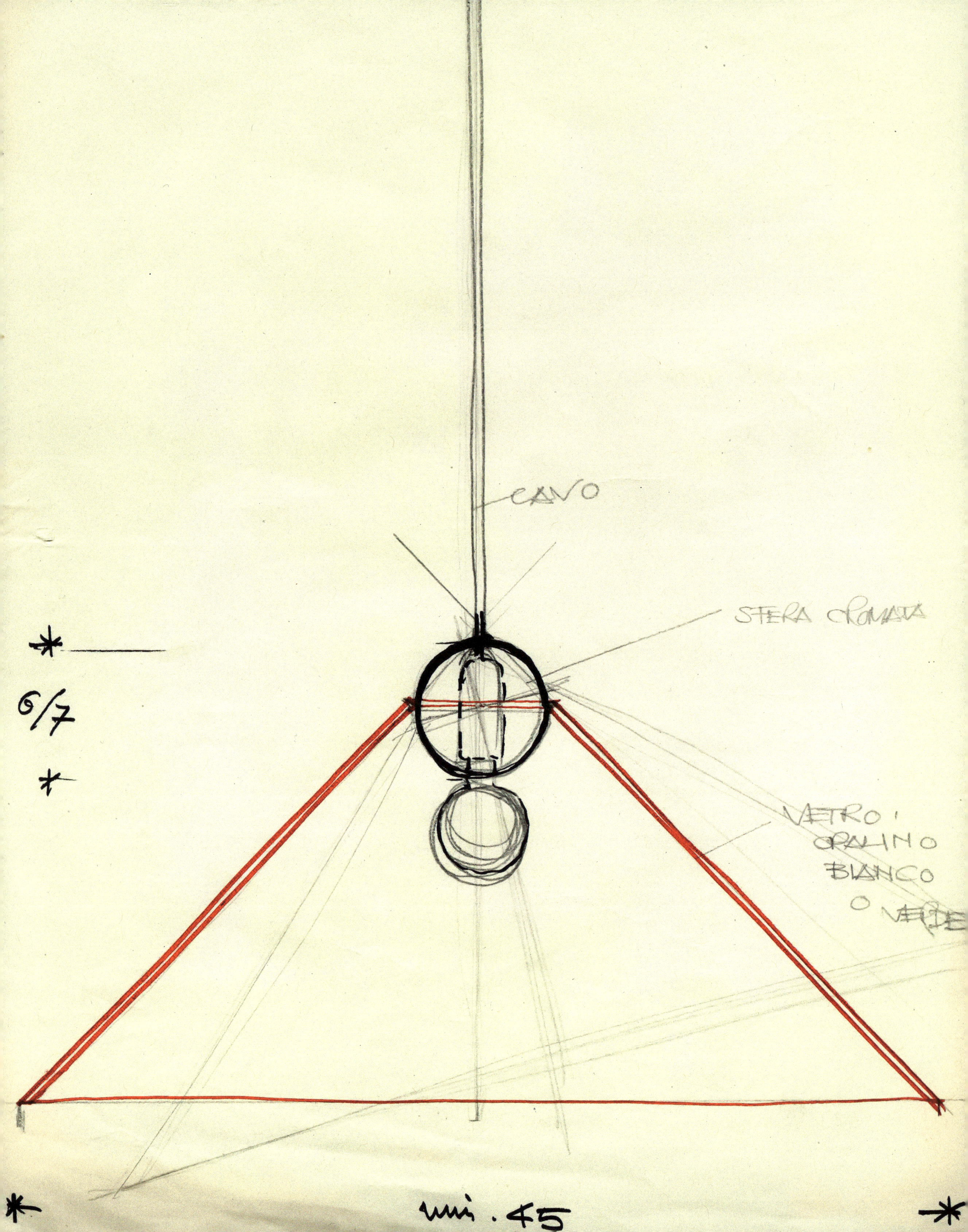
CAVO
STERA CROMATA
VETRO OPALINO BIANCO O VERDE
6/7
m. 45

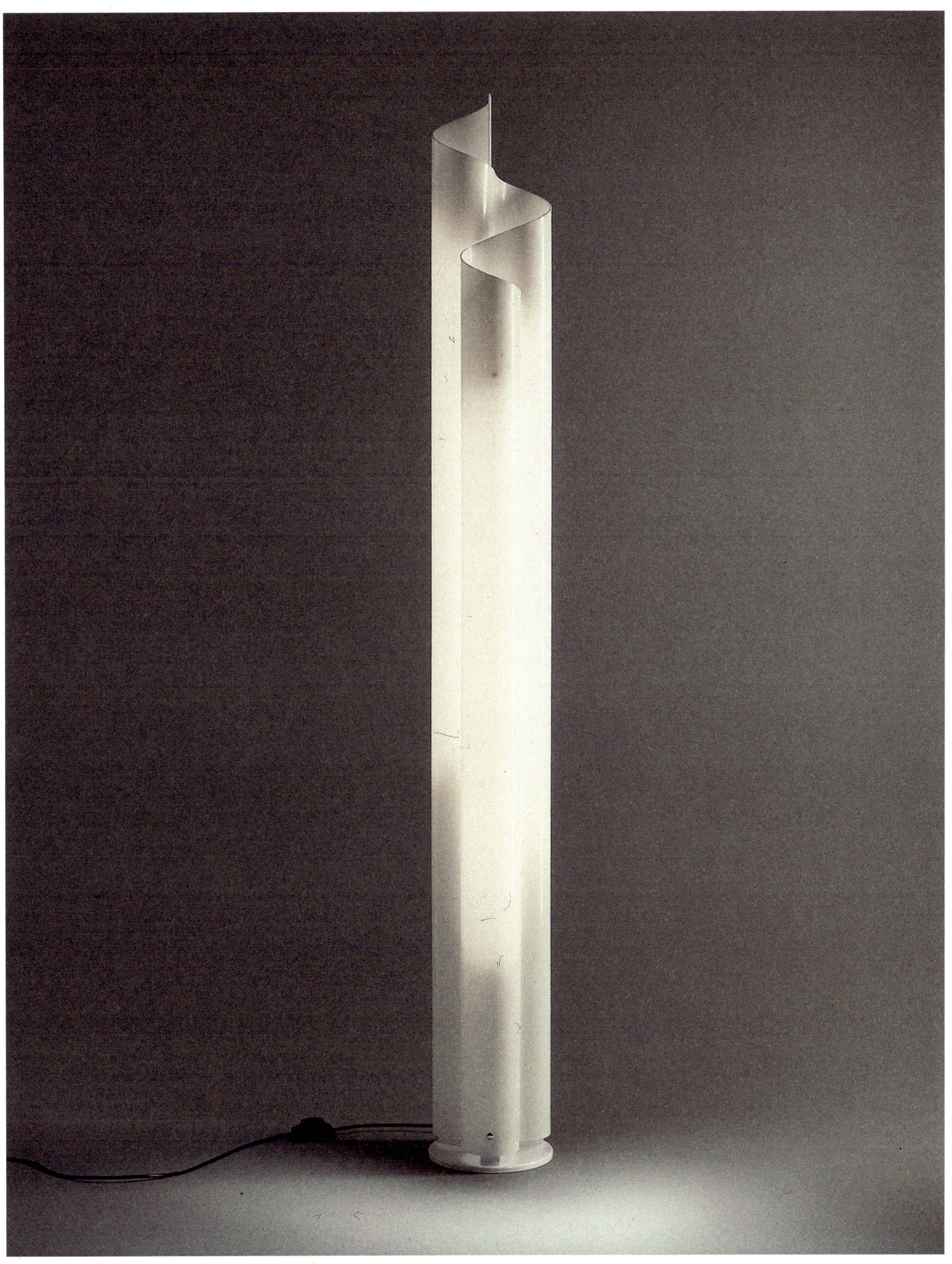

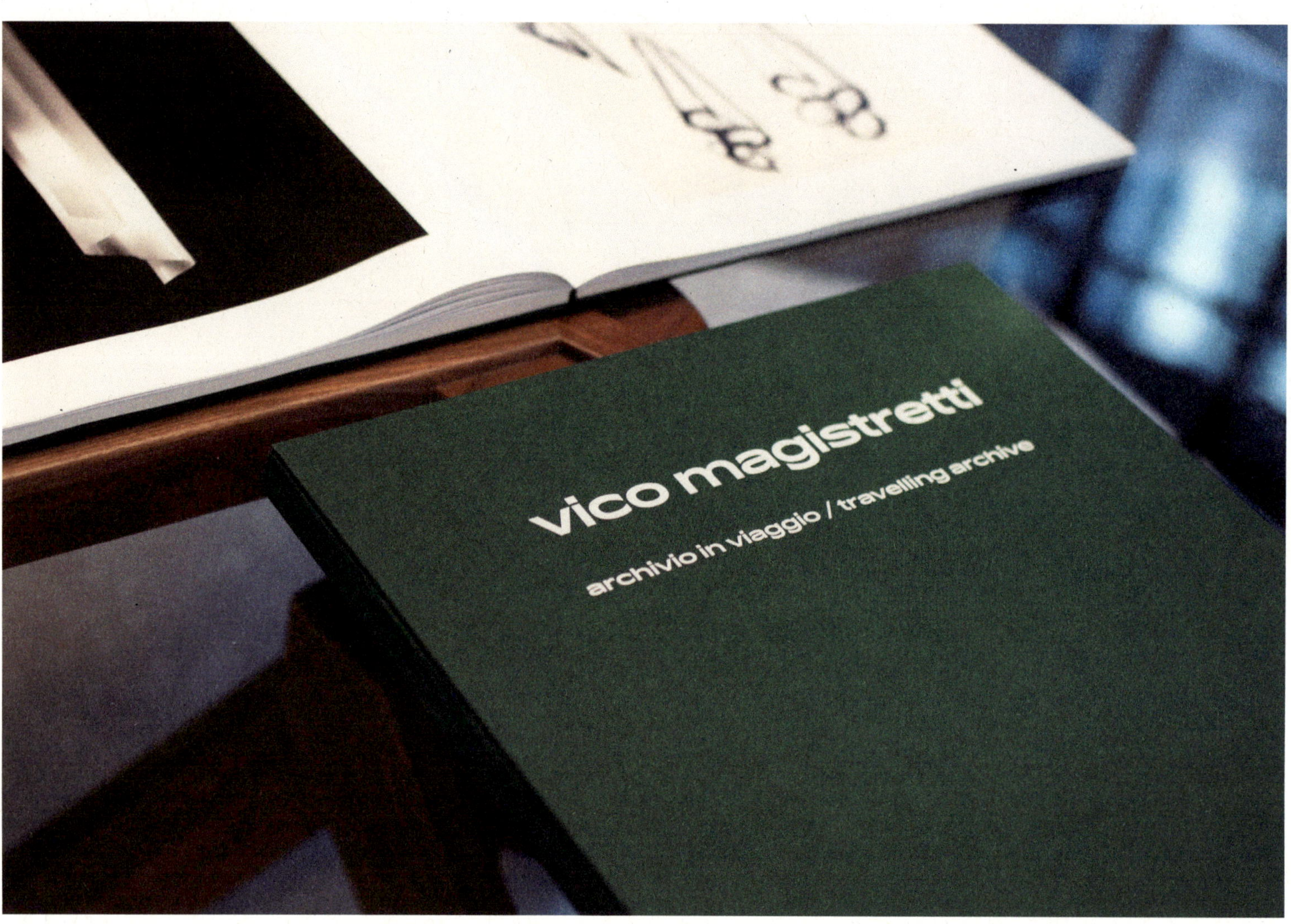
vico magistretti
archivio in viaggio / travelling archive

POLLACK

Euroluce
Vico Magis
Archivio in Viagg
Travelling Archiv

vico
archivio in
travelling

RMIT Design Archives 14.03 – 24.03
vicomagistrettimelbourne.com
@magistretti_melbourne
An exhibition part of Melbourne Design Week 2019, an

gistretti
ggio/
ive
ve by Creative Victoria in partnership with NGV

vico mag

gistretti
Euroluce
Studio opening hours
Monday to Friday
10AM - 5.30PM
T: 03 9657 9657

magistret

Exhibiting Vico Magistretti: The Lesson and Legacy of Conceptual Simplicity

Louise Wright and Mauro Baracco

In 2019 our office Baracco+Wright Architects spent time with the work of Vico Magistretti. Through access to his archive held by the Vico Magistretti Foundation[1] we designed an exhibition for *Vico Magistretti – Archivio in Viaggio/Travelling Archive*. Magistretti consistently came to our assistance. The concepts of primary geometry, simplicity, and play were adopted in ways that we hoped would bring the archive alive.

As an event of the Melbourne Design Week (14-24 March 2019),[2] three 'displays' were designed: one at RMIT Archives reinstalled at the Italian Institute of Culture; an associated window display at RMIT and a shopfront window at the Euroluce showroom in Melbourne.

The idea for this exhibition and its design was simple and straightforward: to group and collect the exhibition content – photos, images, sketches, texts and other material put together by the Magistretti Foundation as an 'archive' of Magistretti's practice[3] – into a large folio that visitors could peruse while at the same time inhabiting a room à la Magistretti, experiencing chairs, lights and a table designed by this Milanese architect.

It is indeed a simple, 'obvious', idea – in a way reflecting the sense of immediateness and essentiality that inform the design approach of Vico Magistretti, constantly inclined to the realisation of products as outcomes of clear and communicable concepts.

At the centre of the exhibition was the archival material which consisted of a reproduction of sketches, snaps of Magistretti and his office which captured a sort of atmosphere and images of a range of the products designed.

The way archives are typically experienced is by sitting down with the material carefully laid out in front of you in a folder or taken from a box. It is immediate and personal, full of discovery that requires close attention. With this in mind we worked with graphic designer Arabella Kilmartin, who has also designed this book, to design a folio of the archival material, so that the visitor could sit down and spend time with it at a table. To make the 'archive' come alive, the folio was placed on a table designed by Magistretti, the round Vidun (1987), with a selection of his chairs – Silver (1989), Uragano (1992) and Pollack (1998) – all produced by De Padova, and under one of his light fittings, the large iteration of the Sonora pendant (1976, Oluce). They needed to be in the room and on the floor, rather than on a pedestal or wall to be able to speak for themselves. The exhibition was completed by the visitor sitting down at the table.

The slightest but definitive separation with the exhibition space was made by positioning the objects on a 20mm Carrara marble 'carpet'. This decision, of taking a precious material and allowing one to walk on it, is very Italian, whose streets are sometimes marble (who could forget the coral and cream coloured marble diagonally striped footpaths off Corso Monforte and Piazza San Babila in Milan). The design of a 'standalone' exhibition also allowed it to be relocated for a few weeks, following the Melbourne Design Week, into a large room at the Italian Institute of Culture in Melbourne.

With only a small range of objects available to us, but more than enough, their arrangement was not chronological, or themed, but simply from smallest to largest, from Teti to Sonora: Teti (1970, Artemide), Eclisse (1967, Artemide), Dalù (1965, Artemide), Mezzachimera (1969, Artemide), Atollo (1977, Oluce) in medium and large, and medium Sonora, and then the table and chairs and large Sonora, all spatially counter-weighted by a stack of Demetrio (1964, Artemide). The sectional progression was reflected in the plan of the marble as a triangle, where the small items were positioned at the pointy end. The triangle was in play with the rectangular room, pushing away from the bossy axis of the building. The large Sonora challenged the high volume of the room peeking its chubby head up into the processional view from the serious and lean hallway.

In the introductory display window facing the street, a Teti lamp dotted each 'i' in a supergraphic 'Vico Magistretti'.

Across town, in the elevated large shopfront window of the showroom for Euroluce, who retail Oluce in Australia, the same sized Sonora and Atollo were positioned side by side with their matching domes aligned, at eye level from the street. An old couple, one with (his) feet on the ground, and one with (her) head in the clouds. Deeper in the space multiple Atollo in different sizes animated the dark room in a play of position and reflection.

Since we had the need to write something about what interests us in our office, we have had a sentence that reappears more or less in the same form: "Our built environments take on simple

1

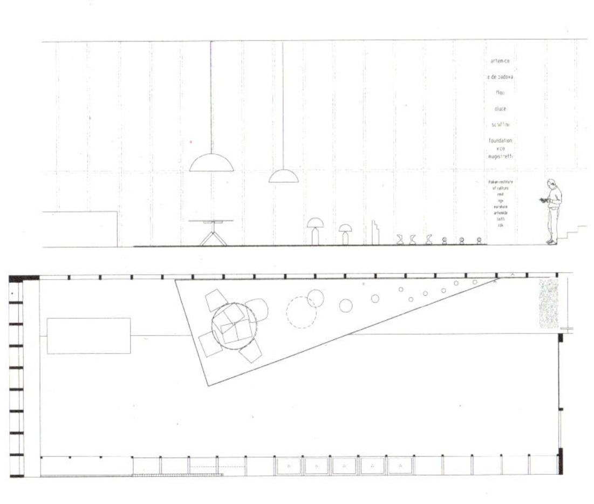

2

3

geometries and restrained material palettes that prioritise the spatial condition and rely on their relationship with landscape."[4]

We are yet to really put our finger on this interest in primary geometrical shapes, diagonal lines, straightforward forms among other things, but observed that without necessarily being bound by them each time, it seemed that's what we are doing. When one finds a similar vein in another's work, the unpacking feels easier, as if, in this case in Vico Magistretti's work, it is reflected back at us.

Differently from some other Italian architects who are obsessively drawn by the detailing – often over detailing – in their design, Magistretti's is fresh and immediate, to the point that some of his works – Chimera lamp among others comes to mind – was 'designed' through discussions over the phone with the maker.[5]

This is indicative of an approach that is intellectual rather than 'architecturally heroic', an approach that believes indeed in the strength of – and collaborative discussions about – ideas rather than in complex and convoluted design (over) performances. An approach that is at the same time confident and humble, firm and gentle, capable to stay open to and embrace the maker's expertise for the realisation of the final product. An anti-heroic approach, capable to freshly operate in negotiating modes, relying on the maker's know-how, a "nimbleness" as Lorenzo Bini describes in his text.

If we think of Magistretti's propension to conceptual simplicity, to essential and geometrical forms rather than mannerist stylistic exercises, it doesn't surprise he was a key figure within that Italian design tradition so often inclined to look at and reinterpret anonymous objects.[6] As we know, anonymous objects are primarily the result of functional rather than stylistic reasons, although not necessarily informed or trapped by functionalist ideologies. In fact in his design and architecture we find Magistretti embedded in his cultural context – things found, come across, remembered and valued.

This generosity of approach in Vico Magistretti's work, manifesting in a kind of familiar

4

5

6

directness often found in pragmatic anonymous objects extended in his hands with a sense of play (through concept, or form, or use), was born from his hope to be free of stylistic concerns:

"I love geometrical forms. I love doing essential things, that look like nothing. To decide is very hard for me, and the idea of a certain definition gives me anguish…but if I choose a cone, then it is a cone. All of a sudden I release myself from stylistic problems".[7]

Primary geometries are simple in a way that can be dogmatic and difficult. But also in a way that can be generous to the designer and user. They afford a sense of control and an anonymity in the shape – 'this is the shape'. They afford a great deal of 'space', air, openness: simple shapes are at once old and new, not concerned with being 'modern', able to absorb shifts in culture and technology. They are the familiar shape of 'normal' things relatively shaped to their task: the funnel, the ruler, a plate. They are also the required ingredient of disquietly 'super normal'[8] things: eye glasses rationally related to the roundness of the eyes while also framing them.

The paradox of the desire to assign the form and quickly move on is after all to assign it utmost importance. In this way the importance is that it leaves potential (rather than dominate or close down) for transformation, relationships, extension and redefinition of existing space and conditions to evolve.

There exists a confidence to embrace a kind of pragmatism: a sloped roof because it is the most effective shelter for protecting against rain, rather than an association of theory with form (for form's sake). The confidence to choose a shape suited to the task at hand, and then move forward seems so crude in approach from other, say more current, approaches to 'creation' where everything is proposed and reproposed free from the human body and its dimensionally related defined elements of doors and rooms, and 'laws' governing construction or composition. One could be accused of being nostalgic. However, in a 'Magistrettian' approach exists an openness for architecture and design to find new relationships. Once the form is released from its own self, we can more easily see its prob-

7

8

lematic relationships in its juxtapositions (for example to the ground, to 'nature', to the non-human) and find possibilities for it to be redefined. Superstudio's geometrical anonymous container put forward in The Continuous Monument (1969-70) could also be considered through this lens.

This position of looking both backwards and forwards is an echo, played out over and over, of the to and fro of let's say 'modern' and 'traditional' that might just be necessary to make breaks and then find our feet again. It has been fruitful for Italian design and architecture. Magistretti's designs for an office building in Corso Europa, Milan and for Villa Arosio in Arenzano, as well as BBPR's Torre Velasca in Milan and Gardella's Olivetti Canteen in Ivrea, all of the same era, broke open an orthodoxy of modernism[9] and delivered us the now famous text by Reyner Banham entitled 'Neoliberty: The Italian Retreat from Modern Architecture'[10] and Rogers' reply in 'The Evolution of Architecture: A Reply to the Refrigerator Keepers'.[11]

We owe a debt to those who have already written about this aspect and the formal and playful qualities in Magistretti's work as discussed in Vanni Pasca's insightful text 'Concepts and Designs'[12] and Gillo Dorfles who observes the "constant application of a design methodology that allows nothing superfluous and insists on compositions of primary forms that have been sectioned, pulled apart and put together again".[13]

A playfulness can be found in the recomposition of Atollo as a series of primary geometric volumes of tube, cone and semi-sphere whose intersection and shape is revealed through illumination as if the sole purpose of the lamp was to show us these shapes; Cirene (1965, Artemide) in its iteration as a floor lamp is a domed shaped hat on a post; Dalù is two opposing semicircles leaning forward to offer light; Chimera (1969, Artemide) is a ribbon like form made possible by the structural integrity of the material (methacrylate); Teti is a celebration of the naked light bulb in a curved cone base reminiscent of a candle holder (or Magistretti said "inkpot"[14]) and composed into a group of

9

10

11

(the magical) three in Triteti (1970, Artemide); Giunone (1969, Artemide) juxtaposes four cut away spheres in a dance of form and light; Impiccato (1970, Artemide) is the most simple of light shade as a dome with a counterweight; Snow (1974, Oluce), whose most pure iteration was probably the pendant – a pure cone; Sonora lamp (1976, Oluce) is a semi sphere or a dome with the subtle use of gold or other more reflective surfaces on the inside of its dome; Porsenna (1976, Artemide) takes the same shape and transforms it in the most simple move that flips the table lamp upside down to create a matching wall lamp – talking to each other when used together and then revisited in Pascal lamp (1979, Oluce) that doubles the cone to create a play of light and reflection; Kuta lamp (1980, Oluce; 1999, Omikron Design; 2015, Nemo) is graphic in its flatness and use of the circular disc diffuser and dome base that is then reversed in Nemea (1979, Artemide) where the disc is again diffuser but now also the base counterweighting the just slightly more than semi spherical lamp hood.

As well, there is a play through use: Maralunga (1973, Cassina) where one moves the head and arm rests;[15] and Eclisse whose light can be hooded.

Cues from traditional and anonymous objects (in the legacy of Rogers this could be said to be very modern) are found consistently in the work; Carimate (1960, Comi; 1963, Cassina; 2001, De Padova) recalling an anonymous English chair but now with red gloss paint finish; Eclisse from a lantern; Sindbad (1981, Cassina), a horse blanket but also feels like a flying carpet and also with a familiarity of the blanket draped over the sofa; Stadio and Selene (1966 and 1969, Artemide) almost a caricature of a table and chair, but in plastic; Nuvola Rossa (1977, Cassina) is a play of diagonal bracing dynamically crossing the verticality of the books; Broomstick series (1979, Alias) derived from anonymous foldable furniture and domestic objects such as clothes and coat stands and basic combinations of 'sticks' recalled in Ospite (1996, Campeggi) – a sofa bed that folds like a card table (and looks like one); Vidun which in Milanese means large screw recalls a traditional work table or

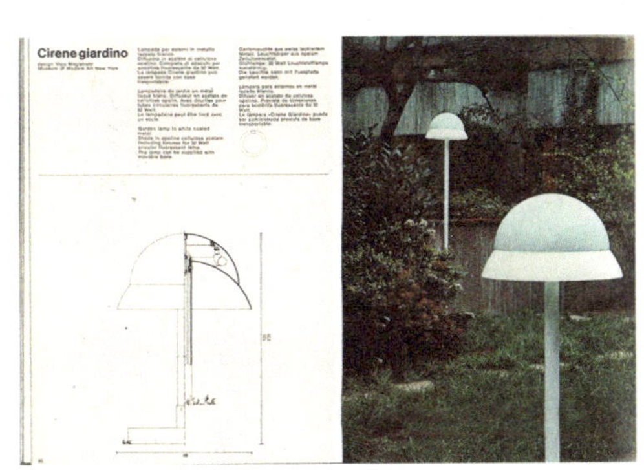

12

13

14

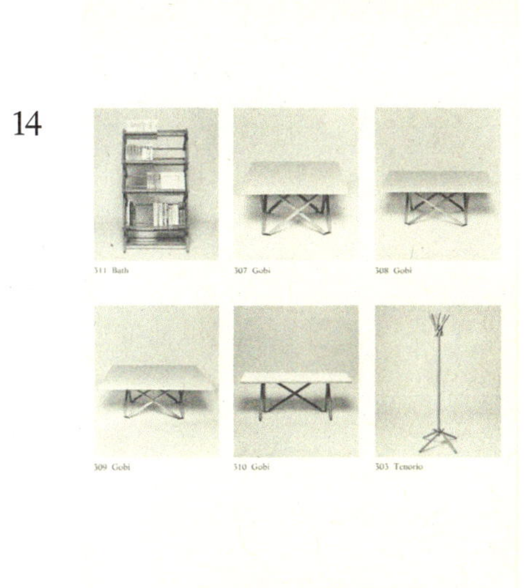

stool and achieves the dream of having multiple heights so invisibly and simply; and Edison (1985, Cassina), a series of tables that use industrial cast iron tube and joint system such as those used by gas companies (i.e. Edison in Milan).

Magistretti's continuous call for simplicity as a fundamental quality for our world[16] is relevant today. As a precursor, well ahead of the many pleas that today invite to work towards the creation of sustainable environments, his approach is not surprisingly in empathy with practices currently inclined to urban and social ecologies informed by levels of 'lightness'. Among others, the call, by contemporary philosopher Leonardo Caffo, for a world that needs to be increasingly released from our weight well echoes Magistretti's fascination for simplicity and lightness:

"If we really want to embrace sustainability as a concrete tenet of daily life and design, we must force ourselves to abandon rhetoric and symbolism and rapidly put into place effective solutions... (shifting) architecture away from the symbolic dimension...and head(ing) toward the concrete dimension of effective change in our relation with the nonhuman environment, with ecosystems... I am imagining the design of lifting the weight of humans on the world, a design that is sustainable because it decreases the load toward we need to carry, instead of strengthening the structure that must carry this weight".[17]

Endnotes

1 See http://www.vicomagistretti.it/en/

2 See https://www.ngv.vic.gov.au/program/vico-magistretti-archivio-in-viaggio-travelling-archive/ and http://vicomagistrettimelbourne.com/ – the latter website, updated for the Melbourne Design Week 2020, refers to and is an extension of the exhibition at the previous Melbourne Design Week 2019.

3 The Fondazione studio museo Vico Magistretti is located in the office space in Milan where Magistretti has practised through all his life.

4 See www.baraccowright.com

5 "...I designed a lamp over the telephone...it's called Chimera, and I explained it to the maker by telephone. I told him, 'Look, make three circles, one, two and three, using this material, which is very easy to bend. Stand it up vertically and cut it at the top by 45 degrees. And then bring it here for me to see'. The model arrived ten days later". Hans Ulrich Obrist, 'Interview with Vico Magistretti', supplement to *Domus*, no. 866, January 2004.

6 Perhaps the fascination with non-designed things from the everyday world may come more naturally to Italians, who since the remote time of the Roman Empire, have never been concerned with imperialist inclinations. In modern/post-medieval times Italy has never been a dominant nation, but rather a country of many different regions constantly invaded and dominated by others. This must have certainly triggered a deep sense of care, of cherishing love, for the many regional, provincial, local cultures – and associated things – in need of shelter, even preservation, under the 'universalist' agendas of the various colonizers (being these French, Austrian, Spanish, Swedish or others).

7 'A colloquio con Magistretti', a conversation between Vico Magistretti and Vanni Pasca, in *Vico Magistretti, Lo studio del genio*, catalogue of an exhibition at the Italian Institute of Culture, Paris, 2014, pp. 35–36; English translation by Mauro Baracco.

8 See Naoto Fukasawa and Jasper Morrison, *Super Normal: Sensations of the Ordinary*, Lars Müller Publishers Zürich, Switzerland, 2007, catalogue of the exhibition *Super Normal* at the Triennale di Milano, 18-23 April 2007, during the Salone Internazionale del Mobile. We note that Vico Magistretti taught at the Royal College of Design in London for twenty years – Jasper Morrison's and Konstantin Grcic's inclination to simplicity and essentiality are undoubtedly indebted to their Milanese teacher and mentor.

9 As noted in Vanni Pasca, *Vico Magistretti: Elegance and Innovation in Postwar Italian Design*, Thames and Hudson, London, UK, 1991, p. 24.

10 Reyner Banham, 'Neoliberty: The Italian Retreat from Modern Architecture', *The Architectural Review*, vol. 125, no. 747, April 1959.

11 Ernesto Nathan Rogers, 'The Evolution of Architecture: A Reply to the Refrigerator Keepers', *Casabella-Continuità*, no. 228, June/July 1959. Vanni Pasca already refers to the confrontation between the English historian and the Italian architect who at that time was also editor of *Casabella-Continuità*; in Vanni Pasca, op. cit., p. 25 and related footnote no. 11, p. 31.

12 Vanni Pasca, 'Concepts and Designs', in *Vico Magistretti: Elegance and Innovation in Postwar Italian Design*, op. cit., pp. 34–49.

13 In Giuliana Gramigna, *Repertorio: 1950-1980*, Mondadori, Milano, Italy, 1985, quoted in ibid, footnote no. 9, p. 49.

14 Beppe Finessi refers to Magistretti's description of this lamp as "a plastic wall fitting made using a simple mold reminiscent of 18th century inkpots"; Beppe Finessi, *Vico Magistretti*, Corraini Editore, Mantova, Italy, 2003, p. 23.

15 Magistretti talks about the play with movement as the main characteristic of this sofa: "(Maralunga is highly successful because of) its extremely soft look, and the magic of movement. People love to know they can move things even if then, perhaps, they never move them", in 'A colloquio con Magistretti', a conversation with Vanni Pasca, op. cit., p. 36; English translation by Mauro Baracco.

16 From an interview with Hans Ulrich Obrist: "HUO: What does a design object need to make it last? VM: Most of all, the most complicated thing in the world: simplicity"; Hans Ulrich Obrist, 'Interview with Vico Magistretti', op. cit.

17 Leonardo Caffo, 'Ecology: the end of rhetoric + an invitation to reality', *Domus/EcoWorld – Design for a healthy planet*, supplement to *Domus*, no. 1027, September 2018.

1 *Vico Magistretti – Archivio in Viaggio/Travelling Archive*, RMIT Design Archives, Melbourne, 2019, photo Ben Hosking

2 *Vico Magistretti – Archivio in Viaggio/Travelling Archive*, plan and elevation, RMIT Design Archives, Melbourne, 2019, Baracco+Wright Architects

3 *Vico Magistretti – Archivio in Viaggio/Travelling Archive*, opening event, RMIT Design Archives, Melbourne, 2019, photo Ramesh Ayyar

4 *Vico Magistretti – Archivio in Viaggio/Travelling Archive*, RMIT Design Archives, Melbourne, 2019, photo Ben Hosking

5 *Vico Magistretti – Archivio in Viaggio/Travelling Archive*, RMIT Design Archives, Melbourne, 2019, photo Ben Hosking

6 Shopfront, Euroluce showroom, Melbourne, 2019, photo Ben Hosking

7 Interior, Euroluce showroom, Melbourne, 2019, photo Ben Hosking

8 *Super Normal* cover

9 Vico Magistretti, Villa Arosio, Arenzano, *Casabella-Continuità*, no. 234, December 1959, cover

10 BBPR, Torre Velasca, Milan, *Casabella-Continuità*, no. 232, October 1959, cover

11 Superstudio, Reflected Architecture, *Casabella*, no. 363, March 1972, cover

12 Cirene giardino, from Artemide catalogue, undated

13 Carimate chairs in Vico Magistretti's office (now Fondazione studio museo Vico Magistretti), Milan, courtesy Fondazione Vico Magistretti, photo Matteo Carassale

14 Broomstick series, Alias, 1979, from Broomstick leaflet

Nimbleness

Lorenzo Bini

Vico Magistretti (1920-2006) knew what he was doing, he knew what he wanted and had no doubts about the role he wanted to play in his profession. He was the son of the architect Pier Giulio Magistretti (1891-1945) and he must have spent his youth – as kids do – observing and studying his father, as a junior challenger who watches and rehearses the moves of a more experienced opponent, planning the whole thing with himself down to the smallest detail. When the time came, he was therefore more than ready to start. It was not simply a matter of architectural language as described in the funny story in which Pier Giulio 'corrects' and enriches with ornaments an excessively modern design by Vico who, however, ignores his father's corrections and shows up for the exam with his own undecorated proposal. Vico must have learnt (by watching his father) what kind of architect he wanted to be, and he became that architect. He knew his place in the project, where his work started and where it should end. He was a designer and not a manager, so he kept his practice very small making use of a single collaborator, the highly trusted draftsman Montella. He must have understood the importance of delegating and the potentials of outsourcing. The building site supervision was not for him. Specifications and bills of quantities? Not his thing. Detailed design and working drawings? No thanks. Interior design? Sorry, can't do that. By precisely defining the borders of his profession Vico could be incredibly productive, completely focused and, most importantly, truly free.

His detachment from the practical duties wasn't at all a strategy to avoid technical problems or necessary compromises but was, on the contrary, a defensive system that provided him with the freedom of focusing on the very essence of things and preserving the strength of his original ideas. By circumscribing his own range of action Vico drew the boundaries of his profession and

1

2

3

between those boundaries he could be suddenly free. This same freedom generated the space that allowed him to effortlessly move between the different scales of the project. He was an architect, but equally an urbanist, a furniture and an industrial designer. He was what AG Fronzoni used to call 'un progettatore', a designer or, if we make a direct unauthorised translation, a 'projectator' able to undertake the design of an entire district or the one of a table lamp with equal effectiveness.

Between teaching and practising he chose the second, at least until teaching became an opportunity to often go to London. He had a precise idea of his city and there was not a single doubt on where to live, where to go and how to move. He was born in a neighbourhood and that was 'his' neighbourhood. He was the son of an architect and he became an architect. He came from a bourgeois family and he remained thoroughly bourgeois. In a way, Vico's life could be ranked as one of those predestined lives. Like the son of a carpenter who is destined to become a carpenter, the blacksmith born into the family business, the factory run by the children of the manufacturer. These lives could be perceived as 'minor lives' or 'marked lives', lives that could have been lived differently if there had been the possibility to choose. But I do love those lives, I think they are incredibly romantic because they go beyond the individual, and I do think there is always a choice. Vico's life was marked by a clear direction and he did, in many ways, continued his own family business. But he decided, he selected and made use of his father's experience. He knew what he wanted and he got it.

Looking at the work of Vico Magistretti today, on the centenary of his birth and with the arduous task in front of me of organising and presenting his endless body of work in a comprehensive exhibition (at Triennale di Milano, 2020), makes me think and rethink the practice of being an architect. In fact putting Vico's life into perspective leaves me with the clear impression that he had an enormous talent in understanding the world around him, his profession, his role, his place, his context and his times. He always wore red socks and there is an ideal thread (in Italy we call it: 'filo

4

5

6

rosso' – 'red thread') that connects and establishes relationships between all his projects, regardless of the scale, the purpose, the client, the location, the discipline and the historical moment. Looking at his Milanese buildings is a particularly useful exercise in this perspective. Vico used to say that when he designed buildings he felt much freer than when he designed objects. At first, I found this statement very confusing because it claimed the opposite of what I would normally think about my profession, which is, you are never free with architecture because you carry the burden of too many constraints and needs. On the contrary, I often think, you can be freer as a furniture designer because you deal with a reduced amount of restrictions and with a limited amount of people, but having the opportunity to know more about the way he interpreted his profession and having taken the time to stop and look at his buildings, I begin to understand what he meant. Vico started building in Milan at the beginning of the 1950s and continued for fifty years. He ventured into different programs, he worked for different clients, he was confronted with different scales and he reacted to different contexts, but his buildings always feature the same clarity and consistency. What they have in common is a sense of primary geometry and simplicity, almost a nimbleness. Vico owed a lot to Ernesto Nathan Rogers and yes, his architecture is deeply modern, but there is more than this. In Magistretti's work it is possible to read a continuity and to identify an evolution at the same time: from the austerity of a church like Santa Maria Nascente (1953-55) – which resembles an industrial prefabricated building – to the compositional severity of the housing in Piazzale Aquileia (1962-64) and Corso di Porta Romana (1962-67); from the mixed-use building in Via San Gregorio (1957-59) – which is not only coeval with the Torre Velasca but also 'Rogersian' in the way it originates from the study of the Lazzaretto – to the houses in Via Conservatorio (1963-66) and Piazza San Marco (1969-71) with their sterner urban graveness already peeking beyond modernity; from the loose volumetric articulation of the Torre al Parco (1953-56) and the house in Via Leopardi (1958-61)

8

7

9

to the repetitive, standardised modularity of the Biology Faculty Building (1978-71) and Famagosta Tram Depot (2000-01). Vico's architectural work is varicoloured but also light because it is the work of a designer who felt, and was, free. His buildings are clear, immediate, pragmatic, simple and essentially Milanese, and Milan, one could say, 'is' his buildings. Sometimes it is as difficult to notice them as it is hard to grasp the fineness of Milan, and they are not necessarily beautiful, because they don't need to be. They are simple, clear and immediate, just like the ideas they originated from. They don't rely on gimmicks hoping to be memorable. They were never fashionable because they were born classics. They make use of simplicity and geometry, stripped of any unnecessary superstructure and they go to the core of architecture. In this sense they are also beautiful, beautiful like the mind that conceived them.

1 Residential and Office Building, Via Leopardi, Milan, 1958-61, photo Lorenzo Bini
2 Mixed-use Building (commercial, office and residential spaces), Piazza San Marco, Milan, 1969-71, photo Lorenzo Bini
3 Residential Building, Corso di Porta Romana, Milan, 1962-67, photo Lorenzo Bini
4 Faculty of Biology, University of Milan, Città Studi area, Milan, 1978-81, photo Lorenzo Bini
5 Residential Building, Piazzale Aquileia, Milan, 1962-64, photo Lorenzo Bini
6 Office Building, Corso Europa, Milan, 1955-57, photo Lorenzo Bini
7 Santa Maria Nascente Church, QT8 area, Milan, 1953-55, photo Lorenzo Bini
8 Residential Building, Via Conservatorio, Milan, 1963-66, photo Lorenzo Bini
9 ATM Tram Depot, Famagosta area, Milan, 2000-01, photo Lorenzo Bini
10 Torre al Parco, Via Revere, Milan, 1953-56, photo Lorenzo Bini
11 Mixed-use Building (residential, office and movie-theatre), Via San Gregorio, Milan, 1957-59, photo Lorenzo Bini

10

11

Restarting from the Sources: The Online Archive of Magistretti's Office

Rosanna Pavoni

To celebrate Vico Magistretti's centenary (1920-2020), the Magistretti Foundation has publicly released the archive of this Milanese architect's office through the portal reachable at the following website: archivio.vicomagistretti.it. More than 30.000 documents are now online, including drawings, sketches, project reports, photographs, correspondence, 450 descriptive files of architecture and design work, 10 thematic profiles – this equates to around 65% of all projects, built and unbuilt, of the actual analogue archive which is located downstairs from the rooms of Vico Magistretti's office that today accommodate the museum/foundation. Therefore, somehow also metaphorically, this archive supports both the inherent history of the exhibited works and the audios with stories of Vico's life and projects from 1946 – when he started working in what it was originally his father's office – to 2006, his death year. Following many years of research, cataloguing and digitising, the archive has now become not only a conservation place but also a generative platform – no longer exclusively a data bank but rather a network place, both 'internally' where Magistretti's activities as architect and industrial designer are never separated, and 'externally' in connection with the Milanese and International cultures of Magistretti's contemporaries.

The *Vico Magistretti – Archivio in Viaggio/Travelling Archive* exhibition held in 2019 at the RMIT Design Archives with the support and contribution of the Italian Institute of Culture in Melbourne and RMIT School of Architecture and Urban Design, aimed to show a speculative process on the archive and the related exhibitions that have been travelling internationally since the Magistretti Foundation began its activities ten years ago (2010-). Through the online platform the aim is now to welcome further contributions, new historical-critical reflections and interpretations, as well as to venture into collaborations with other architecture and design archives in order to produce new visions.

Rosanna Pavoni, Scientific Director, Fondazione studio museo Vico Magistretti

1

Vico Magistretti Between Italy and Australia

Laura Napolitano

As director of the Italian Institute of Culture in Melbourne, it is always a special honour to be part of showcasing Italian excellence of the calibre of Vico Magistretti. In 2019, we organized the beautiful and extremely successful exhibition, *Vico Magistretti – Archivio in Viaggio / Travelling Archive* in collaboration with the RMIT School of Architecture and Urban Design and the RMIT Design Archives. This event fostered a fruitful collaboration between the Institute, RMIT and the Fondazione studio museo Vico Magistretti, and in particular, with the scientific director Rosanna Pavoni. It offered the opportunity to present the complex nature of Italian design to the Australian public: one that has its roots in 20th century history, and yet develops in the peculiar Italian context where design, craftsmanship, mass production and marketing/distribution build a tight system, which sets the standards for contemporary practices and aesthetics at an international level. The exhibition demonstrated the relevance of a figure like Magistretti for present and future designers. The project confirmed that fruitful synergies between countries like Australia and Italy can and should be built also through cultural endeavours.

It is in this spirit that as director of the Italian Institute of Culture I offered my immediate support for the production of this publication, as a permanent way to keep memory of the project alive, but also as an excellent scientific and curatorial tool to engage with the work and legacy of Magistretti: a text which I am sure will become a point of reference for many.

Laura Napolitano, Director of the Istituto Italiano di Cultura, Melbourne, 2017–2020

2

Vico Magistretti at the Design Archives

Harriet Edquist

Design archives are repositories not only of historical data about past design but also of concepts which are timeless. The potential of archives to infiltrate the present with their accumulated store of design ideas is one of their enduring values to contemporary life and so Vico Magistretti's archive, documenting his post-war practice in Milan, Italy, found a welcoming home at the RMIT Design Archives, Melbourne.

Generally, the double height, glazed atrium space or 'active archive' at the Design Archives is where visitors encounter our collections. It occupies the northern face of the award-winning archives building, designed by Melbourne architect Sean Godsell. While exhibitions of post-graduate student work have been held in this space, *Vico Magistretti – Archivio in Viaggio/Travelling Archive* was the first externally-curated exhibition we have ever hosted.

Curators Mauro Baracco and Louise Wright surmounted the challenges presented by the atrium with enormous aplomb. Given a space with glazed walls and far too much light to display original drawings they reconceptualized the archival exhibition. Rather than a static display of drawings pinned to the wall with accompanying text and furniture in attendance, they created a tiny salon.

On a thin triangular sliver of white marble laid across the existing black floor the curators arranged a group of floor lamps, the smallest at the thin end of the triangle, larger ones in the middle and an arrangement of table and chairs at the broad end of the marble. Gathered under two large pendant lights the table and chairs created a space for reading and talking and on the table were two custom-designed folios containing reproductions of the archival drawings. It was an invitation to sit, talk and discuss Magistretti's work both as idea and as object and in so doing, to bring it to life.

Harriet Edquist, Professor of Architectural History at RMIT University and Director of the RMIT Design Archives, Melbourne

1 Vico Magistretti's office (now Fondazione studio museo Vico Magistretti), Milan, courtesy Fondazione Vico Magistretti, photo Matteo Carassale

2 *Vico Magistretti – Archivio in Viaggio/Travelling Archive* exhibition, Italian Institute of Culture, Melbourne, 2019, photo Ramesh Ayyar

3 *Vico Magistretti – Archivio in Viaggio/Travelling Archive* exhibition, RMIT Design Archives, Melbourne, 2019, opening event, photo Ramesh Ayyar

3

Biographies

Mauro Baracco (PhD) is a director of Baracco+Wright Architects (est. 2004) and an Associate Professor at the School of Architecture and Urban Design, RMIT University. His teaching and research have manifested an interest in the local that has developed from historical and cultural to include ecological relationships of the built and unbuilt environment. This activity encompasses design, teaching and philosophy.

Louise Wright (PhD) is a director of Baracco+Wright Architects. Louise and Mauro have taught at various schools including Monash MADA, UTS Sydney; Turin Polytechnic, Italy; Milan Polytechnic, Italy; and Mendrisio Academy of Architecture, Switzerland. Together with Mauro, she is interested in a role for architecture that can extend its relationship with the natural world towards one that supports all life. Recent outcomes of these interests include the publication *Robin Boyd: Spatial Continuity*; Creative Direction of the Australian Pavilion with artist Linda Tegg at the Architecture Venice Biennale 2018 with the theme *Repair*, and built and speculative design projects in collaboration with ecologists, landscape architects and artists.

Lorenzo Bini, architect, was born in 1971. He studied in Milan and Oslo, graduated in 1998 from Politecnico di Milano and worked for different offices in Milan and Rotterdam until 2003 when he began his independent career, at first with a shared partnership named Studiometrico, then later with his own practice: BINOCLE. Lorenzo works on the transformation of existing spaces ranging from temporary structures to permanent buildings and gardens. Beside his professional activity, Lorenzo has been adjunct professor at the Politecnico di Milano, visiting professor at the Design Academy Eindhoven and is currently teaching at Nuova Accademia di Belle Arti in Milan.

Credits

p. 1, Kuta, lamp, Oluce, 1980 (later Omikron Design, 1999; Nemo, 2015), courtesy Oluce
p. 2, Eclisse, lamp, Artemide, 1967, courtesy Artemide
p. 3, Teti, lamp, Artemide, 1970, courtesy Artemide
p. 4, Ospite, bed, Campeggi, 1996, courtesy Campeggi
p. 5, Tenorio, coat rack, Alias 1979 (re-edition Campeggi, 1996), Broomstick series, courtesy Campeggi
pp. 6–7, Nuvola Rossa, bookshelf, Cassina, 1977, courtesy Cassina
pp. 8–9, Maralunga, armchair and sofa, Cassina, 1973, courtesy Cassina
pp. 10–11, Atollo, lamp, Oluce, 1977, courtesy Oluce
p. 13, Edison, table, Cassina, 1985, from Cassina catalogue
pp. 14–15, Vidun, table, De Padova, 1987, courtesy De Padova, photo Luciano Soave
p. 16–17, Selene, chair, Artemide, 1969, from 'È nata una sedia', *Ottagono*, no. 15, October 1969
p. 19, Sindbad, armchair and sofa, Cassina, 1981, courtesy Cassina
p. 20, Monet, lamp, Oluce, 1980, courtesy Oluce
p. 21, Monet, lamp, Oluce, 1980, courtesy Oluce
p. 22, Pascal, lamp, Oluce, 1979, courtesy Oluce
p. 23, Pascal, lamp, Oluce, 1979, courtesy Oluce
p. 24, Sonora, lamp, Oluce, 1976, courtesy Oluce
p. 25, Sonora, lamp, Oluce, 1976, sketch, courtesy Archivio Studio Magistretti, Fondazione Vico Magistretti
p. 26, Snow, lamp, Oluce, 1974, sketch, courtesy Archivio Studio Magistretti, Fondazione Vico Magistretti
p. 27, Snow, lamp, Oluce, 1974, courtesy Oluce
p. 28, Snow, lamp, Oluce, 1974, courtesy Oluce
p. 30, Pan, chair, Rosenthal Studio Linie, 1980, courtesy Rosenthal
pp. 32–33, Cina, kitchen, Schiffini Mobili Cucine, 1986, courtesy Schiffini
p. 35, Chimera, lamp, Artemide, 1969, courtesy Artemide
p. 37, Blossom, table, De Padova, 2002, courtesy De Padova, photo Luciano Soave
pp. 38–49, *Vico Magistretti – Archivio in Viaggio/Travelling Archive* exhibition, RMIT Design Archives, Melbourne Design Week 2019, photo Ben Hosking
pp. 50–53, Installation at Euroluce showroom, Melbourne, Melbourne Design Week 2019, photo Ben Hosking

Title
Geometry, Simplicity, Play: Exhibiting Vico Magistretti

Published by
Actar Publishers, New York, Barcelona
www.actar.com

Authors
Louise Wright and Mauro Baracco, Baracco+Wright Architects

Graphic Design
Arabella Kilmartin

With contributions by
Lorenzo Bini, Rosanna Pavoni, Laura Napolitano, Harriet Edquist

Printing and binding
DZA Druckerei zu Altenburg GmbH

Distribution
Actar D, Inc. New York, Barcelona.

New York
440 Park Avenue South, 17th Floor
New York, NY 10016, USA
salesnewyork@actar-d.com

Barcelona
Roca i Batlle 2-4
08023 Barcelona, Spain
eurosales@actar-d.com

Indexing
English ISBN: 978-1-94876-552-7
PCN: Library of Congress Control Number: 2020932522

Printed in Germany
Publication date: March 2020

Number One, 2020

This book acknowledges the Wurundjeri people of the Kulin Nations as the traditional owners of the land upon which the previous exhibition and production of this book have taken place.

A partnership between Istituto Italiano di Cultura, Melbourne; RMIT University, School of Architecture and Urban Design; Fondazione studio museo Vico Magistretti, Milan. It documents the previous exhibition *Vico Magistretti - Archivio in Viaggio/Travelling Archive*, Melbourne, 2019, an event part of Melbourne Design Week 2019, an initiative by Creative Victoria in partnership with National Gallery of Victoria (NGV), into an extended discussion to celebrate Vico Magistretti (1930-2006) in his centenary year (2020). We acknowledge the industry partners that collaborated with the exhibition: Boffi | De Padova Studio (Sydney and Melbourne), Euroluce Australia, Artemide Australia, CDK Stone, Adriatic Stone with the support of RMIT Design Archives, RMIT Design Hub Gallery, Lockrey Shewan Collection.

vicomagistrettimelbourne.com
@magistretti_melbourne

Thank you to Rosanna Pavoni and Margherita Pellino of the Fondazione studio museo Vico Magistretti, Laura Napolitano of the Istituto Italiano di Cultura (Melbourne), Harriet Edquist of RMIT Design Archives, Lorenzo Bini and Arabella Kilmartin. Thank you to the producers and photographers of Vico Magistretti's work who kindly permitted use of their images.